The Making of Everyday Things

Ice Cream

Derek Miller

New York

Published in 2020 by Cavendish Square Publishing, LLC
243 5th Avenue, Suite 136, New York, NY 10016

Copyright © 2020 by Cavendish Square Publishing, LLC

First Edition

No part of this publication may be reproduced, stored in a retrieval system, or transmitted in any form or by any means—electronic, mechanical, photocopying, recording, or otherwise—without the prior permission of the copyright owner. Request for permission should be addressed to Permissions, Cavendish Square Publishing, 243 5th Avenue, Suite 136, New York, NY 10016. Tel (877) 980-4450; fax (877) 980-4454.

Website: cavendishsq.com

This publication represents the opinions and views of the author based on his or her personal experience, knowledge, and research. The information in this book serves as a general guide only. The author and publisher have used their best efforts in preparing this book and disclaim liability rising directly or indirectly from the use and application of this book.

All websites were available and accurate when this book was sent to press.

Library of Congress Cataloging-in-Publication Data

Names: Miller, Derek, author.
Title: Ice cream / Derek Miller.
Description: First edition. | New York : Cavendish Square, 2020. | Series: The making of everyday things |
Includes bibliographical references and index. | Audience: Grades K to 3.
Identifiers: LCCN 2018048429 (print) | LCCN 2018048949 (ebook) | ISBN 9781502646934 (ebook) | ISBN 9781502646927 (library bound) |
ISBN 9781502646903 (pbk.) | ISBN 9781502646910 (6 pack)
Subjects: LCSH: Ice cream, ices, etc.--Juvenile literature.
Classification: LCC TX795 2020 (ebook) | LCC TX795 .M637 2020 (print) | DDC 641.86/2--dc23
LC record available at https://lccn.loc.gov/2018048429

Editorial Director: David McNamara
Copy Editor: Nathan Heidelberger
Associate Art Director: Alan Sliwinski
Designer: Ginny Kemmerer
Production Coordinator: Karol Szymczuk
Photo Research: J8 Media

The photographs in this book are used by permission and through the courtesy of: Cover Shaiith/Shutterstock.com; p. 5 Tom Wang 112/iStockphoto.com; p. 7 Olga Miltsova/iStockphoto.com; p. 9 Shorrocks/iStockphoto.com; p. 11 Tatiana Gorbunova/Shutterstock.com; p. 13 Vitalii Petrushenko/Shutterstock.com; p. 15 Volkreich/Ullstein Bild/Getty Images; p. 17 Socrates 471/iStockphoto.com; p. 19 Photononstop/Alamy Stock Photo; p. 21 Ross Helen/iStockphoto.com.

Printed in the United States of America

Contents

Ice Cream **4**

New Words **22**

Index **23**

About the Author **24**

Ice cream is a dessert.

It is cold and creamy.

People around the world eat it.

Ice cream has many **ingredients**.

Each ingredient is important.

They make ice cream tasty.

Milk is the most important ingredient.

Milk comes from cows.

Ice cream is mostly milk.

9

Cream is fat from milk.

Cream is added to milk to make ice cream.

Cream makes ice cream tastier.

Ice cream needs sugar.

Sugar makes ice cream sweeter.

Sugar is added to the milk and cream.

13

The milk, cream, and sugar are **churned**.

Churning is like stirring.

Special **paddles** churn the ice cream.

15

Churning adds air to the ice cream.

Air makes the ice cream fluffy.

Ice cream needs air in it.

When it is churning,
ice cream is frozen.

Freezing the ice cream
keeps the air in it.

Freezing it also makes it
so cold!

Flavors are added to ice cream.

Chocolate and vanilla are flavors.

Ice cream is a tasty treat!

New Words

churned (CHURND) Stirred and mixed.

flavors (FLAY-vers) Things that are added to change the taste.

ingredients (in-GREE-dee-entz) The things needed to make something.

paddles (PAD-uls) Tools that churn.

Index

air, 16, 18

churned, 14, 16, 18

cold, 4, 18

cream, 10, 12, 14

flavors, 20

ingredients, 6, 8

milk, 8, 10, 12, 14

paddles, 14

sugar, 12, 14

tasty, 6, 10, 20

About the Author

Derek Miller is a teacher and writer. He likes to learn interesting facts about things we see every day.

About

Bookworms help independent readers gain reading confidence through high-frequency words, simple sentences, and strong picture/text support. Each book explores a concept that helps children relate what they read to the world they live in.